OUR ANGRY PLANET

Floods

ANNE ROONEY

Adapted from an original text by Anita Ganeri

FRANKLIN WATTS
LONDON•SYDNEY

First published in 2009 by Franklin Watts

Copyright © 2009 Arcturus Publishing Limited

Franklin Watts
338 Euston Road
London NW1 3BH

Franklin Watts Australia
Level 17/207 Kent Street, Sydney, NSW 2000

Produced by Arcturus Publishing Limited,
26/27 Bickels Yard, 151–153 Bermondsey Street, London SE1 3HA

Our Angry Planet is based on the series *Nature's Fury*, published by Franklin Watts.

Editor: Alex Woolf
Designer: Mind's Eye Design and Mike Reynolds

Picture Credits
Corbis: 8 (Reuters/Jayanta Shaw), 11 (George H. H. Huey), 12 (Alberto Pizzoli), 16 (Kjeld Duits/epa), 17 (Kapoor Baldev/Sygma), 18 (Alessandro della Bella/epa), 20 (Howard Davies), 22 (Sergey Ilnitsky/epa), 23 (Bettmann), 24 (Themba Hadebe/epa), 25 (John Gress/Reuters), 26 (Elvis Barukcic/epa), 29 (Alexandra Winkler/Reuters).
NASA Visible Earth: 9, 19 (Jacques Descloitres, MODIS Rapid Response Team, NASA/GSFC).
Rex Features: 4 (Sipa Press), 5 (Stewart Cook), 10 (Sipa Press), 13 (Sipa Press), 15 (Sipa Press), 21 (The Travel Library), 27 (Nicholas Bailey).
Science Photo Library: 6 (Gary Hincks), 7 (Wayne Lawler), 14 (Carlos Munoz-Yague/LDG/Eurelios), 28 (Paul Rapson).
Shutterstock: cover (egd).

Every attempt has been made to clear copyright. Should there be any inadvertent omission, please apply to the publisher for rectification.

A CIP catalogue record for this book is available from the British Library.

Dewey Decimal Classification Number: 551.48'9

ISBN 978 0 7496 9047 2

Printed in China

Franklin Watts is a division of Hachette Children's Books, an Hachette UK Company
www.hachette.co.uk

Contents

What is a Flood?   4

Flowing Rivers   6

Flood Patterns   8

Flash Floods   10

Coastal Flooding   12

Tsunami Flooding   14

Human-Made Floods   16

Changing the Landscape   18

Living with Floods   20

Effects of Flooding   22

Rescue and Recovery   24

Flood Protection   26

Flood Prediction   28

Ten of the Deadliest Floods   30

Further Information   30

Glossary   31

Index   32

What is a **Flood?**

A flood happens when water from a river or sea covers the land. Floods may be caused by heavy rain swelling rivers until water pours over the land. They may also happen when storms send huge waves crashing over the coast. Floods can destroy towns and farmland and drown people.

▼ A flood in Germany in 2002 was caused by the River Elbe overflowing.

Killer floods

Floods happen more often than other natural disasters such as earthquakes, famines and volcanic eruptions. They kill more people, too. Through history, tens of millions of people have died in floods, and a large flood can kill millions at once. Fast flowing flood waters wash away buildings, cars, roads and even the soil.

Flood types

There are three types of flood. A river flood happens when a river fills up and the water overflows onto the land. Flash floods happen when lots of rain falls over a small area. Coastal floods happen when storms and big waves bring seawater pouring over the land.

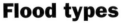

Floods can be good for farming. The soil near rivers that flood is very good for growing crops. This makes the land around the rivers a good place to live, even though the floods can be dangerous.

◄ In New Orleans, USA, Hurricane Katrina caused deep floods in 2005.

 ## THE BIBLICAL FLOOD

There are many legends about a very big flood, long ago. In the Bible, God sends a flood to cover the Earth. Only Noah and his family survive. The legends may be based on a real flood that happened 5,000 years ago.

Flowing Rivers

The amount of water on Earth does not change. The water moves between the sea, the air and the land. Water **evaporates** from the sea and the land and forms clouds. The water vapour in the clouds falls as rain. Some rain falls on the land and runs into rivers and the sea. Then it evaporates again. This is called the **water cycle**.

▼ Water evaporates from the sea and falls as rain over the mountains. It flows in a river back to the sea.

Soaking in and running off

Rain falling on the land can soak in or run over the ground. When it runs over the ground it is called **run-off**. On some types of soil, water cannot soak in easily. When rain falls too quickly to soak in, or if the ground is already too wet, the rain runs off.

Forming a floodplain

Water flows downhill. It collects in streams and rivers. These slowly eat into the ground, making V-shaped valleys.

They carry soil and rock along with them. This is dropped when the river slows down over flat ground. In low-lying areas, the river bends from side to side. Over many years, it makes a wide valley. When there is too much water in the river, the wide valley floods. This is the **floodplain**.

GROUNDWATER

Water that soaks into the ground is called **groundwater**. When there is a lot of groundwater, the ground becomes **saturated**. The top saturated layer is the **water table**. Groundwater leaks out of the water table to form springs. The water flows into streams and rivers. Groundwater keeps rivers flowing even in dry weather.

▲ The River Bynoe in Australia winds through its floodplain. The floodplain is made from soil and rock left behind by floods.

Flood Patterns

Rivers often flood at the same time each year. These are seasonal floods. They are caused by rain, storms or melting snow. They happen at different times in different places. In South-East Asia seasonal floods happen in summer when there is heavy rain. Rivers carry up to 20 times more water during this wet season.

One-off floods

Some floods do not follow a regular pattern. These are one-off floods. Some rivers flood after very heavy rain only every few years. Scientists label these floods according to how often they happen. A ten-year flood happens about once every ten years.

▶ Monsoon rains caused these floods in Guwahati in India in 2000.

A 100-year flood happens about once in a 100 years, and is far more serious. **Tropical cyclones** are whirling storms that form over the sea. They create one-off storms by dropping huge amounts of rain very quickly.

Flood surges

A flood does not happen as soon as the rain starts. It can take a long time for water to build up in a river and flow downstream to where a flood happens. The flood can be hundreds of kilometres from the area where the rain fell. It may happen hours or even days after the storm that caused it.

▲ A tropical cyclone over the Indian Ocean. Cyclones cause flooding on coasts and rivers.

 CASE STUDY

China, 1931

In a summer **monsoon**, lots of rain falls over a few months. In southern China, monsoon rains flow into two large rivers, the Huang Ho (Yellow River) and Chiang Jang (Yangtze). These rivers often flood after the monsoon. In 1931 terrible flooding killed nearly five million people along these rivers.

Flash Floods

A flash flood is a sudden, quick flood. It happens when slow-moving storm clouds cause extremely heavy rain. The water follows the quickest route downhill. It may flow through a valley or though a town or city.

▼ People may be washed off their feet in flash floods like this one, in Istanbul in Turkey.

Storm clouds

The storm clouds that cause flash floods can be ten kilometres tall. They grow when hot, wet air rises. Air swirls up and down inside the clouds. It carries droplets of water with it. The droplets grow larger and heavier until they fall as rain. Sometimes the whole cloud collapses. Hundreds of thousands of tonnes of rain can fall in a few minutes. This is called a **cloudburst**.

Where flash floods happen

Flash floods can happen if a river is too short to cope with a sudden heavy flow of water. They also happen when rain falls on ground that is already waterlogged. They can even happen in deserts if enough rain falls. In towns and cities, water can't always drain away quickly. It can't soak into the hard surfaces of roads and pavements.

CASE STUDY

▲ Even deserts can have flash floods. This one is in the Valley of the Gods in Utah, USA.

Boscastle, UK, 2004

A flash flood wrecked the village of Boscastle in England in 2004. On a warm August day, 75 millimetres of rain fell in two hours. A raging torrent up to three metres deep flooded the streets from two rivers. Houses and cars were destroyed. Luckily, no one died. Experts say such a flood would happen once in 400 years in Boscastle.

Coastal Flooding

Land along the coast is often only a few metres above the level of the sea. It may even be below sea level. Storms and high tides can cause the sea level to rise. Sometimes it floods the land. The sea can also flow up rivers, causing floods.

▼ In autumn, Venice often floods at high tide. Up to two-thirds of the city streets may be underwater.

Storm surges

When storms cause sea levels to rise, they create a **storm surge**. In a storm the air pressure is lower than normal. The force of the air pressing down on the sea is smaller than usual. This means the sea is sucked upwards a little, so the sea level rises. The largest storm surges are caused by **cyclones**. They can raise the water level by five metres or more.

Areas at risk

Millions of people live along the coasts where floods may happen. Some major cities, such as London, are only a few metres above sea level.

Low-lying islands may disappear underwater in coastal floods. The city of Venice in Italy is built on 120 islands and often floods in storms. A fifth of the Netherlands is below sea level. The land has been drained and is surrounded by earth banks called **dykes**.

▲ Only the roofs of houses are visible above flood waters in New Orleans.

CASE STUDY

New Orleans, USA, 2005

The city of New Orleans in the USA was badly flooded in August 2005. The flood was caused by a storm surge from Hurricane Katrina. The surge pushed extra water into a lake near the city until the flood barriers collapsed. Three-quarters of New Orleans flooded. In some places, the water was six metres deep.

Tsunami Flooding

Tsunami is a Japanese word. It means 'harbour wave'. A tsunami travels very quickly across the ocean as a low wave. When it reaches the coast, it grows taller and pours inland.

How tsunamis start

▼ A computer model shows how a landslide under the sea makes the water above move, causing a tsunami.

Tsunamis are usually caused by earthquakes under the sea. If the seabed rises or falls, water is pushed up or falls down. Landslides under the sea or volcanic eruptions can also cause tsunamis. In 1883 the volcano Krakatau in Indonesia erupted. Tsunamis up to 40 metres high flooded nearby islands.

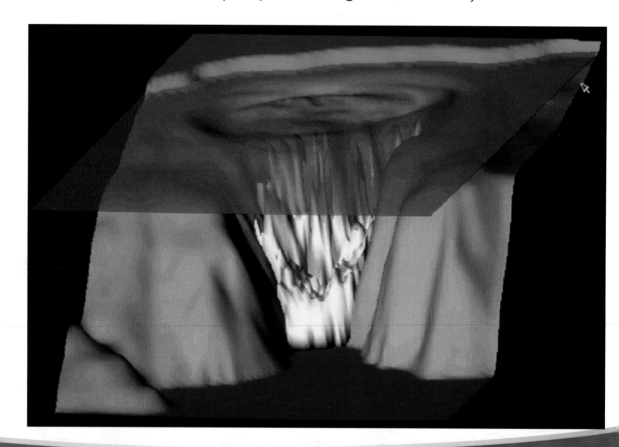

How tsunamis travel

A tsunami makes rings of waves that spread out in all directions. They move as fast as a jet airliner. The waves are just a few metres high, but can be hundreds of kilometres apart. They may hit land thousands of kilometres from where they started. The waves slow down in the shallow water near the coast. They get closer together and larger. On the shore, the sea level drops quickly. It is the first sign that a tsunami is coming. Then the sea pours back in as giant waves flood the land.

▲ This photograph was taken a day after the tsunami hit the city of Banda Aceh in Indonesia in 2004.

CASE STUDY

Asian tsunami, 2004

A huge earthquake happened under the sea in the Indian Ocean on 26 December 2004. It was the second most powerful earthquake ever recorded. It caused a tsunami that devastated parts of Thailand, Sri Lanka and India. The waves grew up to 30 metres tall as they came near the shore. Towns and villages were flattened and more than 283,000 people died.

Human-Made **Floods**

Most floods happen naturally, but some are caused by people. They often happen when stored water escapes. In the future, **climate change** will lead to more floods. Human beings cause **global warming** by burning fuels such as gas and oil. This leads to climate change, so these floods will be our fault.

Dam bursts

Dams are barriers that block rivers. They are made to store water or to stop flooding. Sometimes dams fall down. The water then pours out, flooding the valleys below. A dam may break if it

▼ **Floods caused by Typhoon Togake broke this Japanese dam in 2004. The water from the breaking dam made the flood even worse.**

was badly built or if it is damaged by earthquakes or floods. Some experts think giant dams built to stop floods may lead to disasters.

Deliberate floods

A **reservoir** is a large store of water that people use for their water supply. Some reservoirs are made by building a dam and flooding the land behind it. This stops the flow of a river. Floods are sometimes even used as weapons in war. Chinese soldiers started a flood in 1938 to stop a Japanese invasion. British aircraft bombed two dams in Germany in 1943 to flood an important industrial area.

▲ These people in India were made homeless when their villages were flooded by dams on the River Narmada.

CASE STUDY

St Francis Dam, USA, 1928

The St Francis Dam in California, USA, was made in 1926 to supply water to Los Angeles. The reservoir was filled in 1928. Engineers were not worried when they found cracks in the concrete as they thought it was still safe. The dam collapsed a few days later. Water 38 metres deep crashed into the valley. More than 400 people died.

Changing the Landscape

Rivers wear away the land in a process called erosion. During a flood, erosion increases. Flood waters tear soil and rock from the riverbed and banks and drop it on the **floodplain**. Floods completely change the course of a river

Erosion

Flood water is very powerful. Flash floods wash huge boulders downstream, crashing them into the bank and riverbed. The sides of steep valleys may collapse in landslides and mudslides. In dry areas, heavy rain washes the soil away and cuts deep gullies in the landscape.

▶ Other houses near this one were destroyed when a flash flood **eroded** the land in this street in Switzerland in 2005.

Dropping the load

The water in a flooded river is turned brown by the **sediment** it carries. Some sediment falls to the riverbed, making the river shallower. Some is carried to the floodplain or builds up along the riverbank. Where the river meets the sea, dropped sediment makes a **delta**.

Effects on plants

Flood water can rip plants from the ground or strip them bare. Flash floods and **tsunamis** can even pull trees out of the ground. Standing flood waters and salt from seawater flooding kill plants. But in deserts floods are sometimes needed to help seeds to start growing. The seeds may lie in the ground for years before a flood comes.

▲ This photograph from space shows green areas where plants have grown after summer flooding in Australia.

PLANTS STOP EROSION

Plant roots hold the soil in place, so water can soak into the ground. The roots also take in water. This helps to dry out the soil. When plants are removed, the rain runs off. Flash floods then wash away the soil.

Living with **Floods**

Hundreds of millions of people live in areas at risk of floods. Why do they do it? Some have no choice. The only land available is on the **floodplain**. But there are advantages to living in areas that flood.

▶ **These houses in Bangladesh are built on stilts to keep them above flood waters.**

Good for growing

The **sediment** dropped on floodplains is full of minerals that plants need to grow. It makes the soil on the floodplain good for growing food crops. The river is also useful for watering the plants. But when a flood comes it destroys a whole year's crop.

Flooded fields

Rice is a type of grass. It grows best in fields that are flooded for part of the year. In Asia, farmers grow rice in fields called **paddies**. The **monsoon** rains flood the paddies. Earth banks built around the paddies hold the water in.

More advantages

Cities are often built near rivers. The river provides water, and goods can be moved along the river by boat. In richer countries, people like to live by rivers so that they can go fishing and boating. People live along the coast to make a living from fishing in the sea.

▲ Farmers plant rice in Vietnam. They need the floods to grow their crop.

CASE STUDY

Bangladesh, 1991

Bangladesh has regular river floods and **cyclones**. Four-fifths of the country is made of floodplains and **deltas**. Millions of farmers live in areas that often flood. In 1991 a cyclone caused severe flooding in Bangladesh. About 140,000 people died and 1.5 million lost their homes. Millions of tonnes of crops were ruined.

Effects of **Flooding**

When a flood strikes, people are at risk of drowning in fast-flowing water. The risk is greatest in flash floods and **tsunamis**. A tsunami can sweep people inland and then drag them out to sea. They may be injured by debris carried by the water. Developing countries are often not prepared for floods. The effects can be devastating.

▼ Even shallow flood water like this in Kemerovo in Russia will do much harm to a home.

Damaged homes

Fast-flowing floods can crash through buildings and sweep them away. If floods **erode** the ground, buildings may fall down. Wooden buildings sometimes float away. Water that rises slowly seeps into plaster and damages houses and furniture. Stinking mud and rubbish are left behind after the water has gone. Cars can be washed away and wrecked. Coastal floods carry boats inland where they are smashed.

Water everywhere

Fast-flowing water pushes over the supports of bridges and lifts roads from underneath. Underground, water floods electricity mains, cables and gas pipes. Gas leaks are dangerous, and so is water reaching live electricity cables. Basements and other underground spaces flood. Drains and sewers fill with water and dirty water floods the street. This is dangerous to health.

▲ When trains are damaged by floods, it can take weeks to get the railway system working again.

DAMAGE TO FARMS

In developing countries, floods hit farmers hard. They lose crops, animals, seeds for planting and stored food. Their farmland and systems for watering crops are damaged. Farmers and their families lose everything and have no money or food to live on. In small countries that need to export food, floods can mean the whole country is poor.

Rescue and Recovery

▼ Soldiers and sailors often help in disasters. This sailor in the South African navy is helping a child in the flooded Zambezi River.

The first task for the emergency services in a flood is to rescue people. People can easily drown in their cars, which sink in water. Half the people who die in flash floods in the USA die in their cars. People who go to the tops of buildings or into trees must be rescued quickly if flood waters are rising.

Finding shelter

People made homeless by floods need food, shelter and drinking water until they can go home. Floods often damage water supplies. Drinking dirty water makes people ill, so it is important to supply clean water for them to drink. In developing countries, aid agencies often have to help. Aid agencies help in the longer term if crops are damaged and people are at risk of starvation.

Cleaning up

When flood waters start to go down, it's time to clean up. It can take months to repair homes so that people can move back in. Standing water is pumped back into rivers. This is especially important in hot countries where the water can become home to mosquitoes. These carry the deadly disease **malaria**.

CASE STUDY

New Orleans, 2005

Thousands of people were trapped in buildings and on roofs when New Orleans was flooded in 2005. The USA is one of the richest countries in the world, but it took four days to begin a proper rescue operation. Hundreds of people died, but many could have been saved by better planning and a quicker rescue response.

Flood Protection

People have tried to protect their homes and farms from floods for thousands of years. Today, we stop water from escaping from rivers or flowing inland from the coast by building barriers. We can also cut down the amount of water in a river so that it is less likely to overflow.

▲ Flood water is being let out through this dam to prevent the reservoir from flooding.

Embankments

Embankments are walls built along each side of a river to stop water overflowing onto the **floodplain**. They are often called **levees**. To stop flooding downstream, some water is diverted or stored in lakes for a while. It can be directed onto part of the floodplain to protect other parts.

Delaying a flood

Dams can be used to stop rivers from flooding. Water builds up behind the dam in a **reservoir**. The water level is controlled carefully. Water is let out slowly, so that it does not cause a flood.

Preventing floods by the sea

Embankments called **dykes** help to hold back the sea. A long line of dykes and **barrages** protects the Netherlands. Barrages are gates built across an **estuary**. When the gate is open, water flows into the sea. If there is a **storm surge**, the gates are closed. This stops seawater from flowing up the river and flooding the land.

▲ The Thames Flood Barrier in London closes when there is a storm surge. It stops seawater from flooding low-lying parts of the city.

 PROTECT OR NOT?

Some flood experts think stopping a river from overflowing onto its floodplain will cause floods downstream. They say protecting the floodplain makes people more likely to build on it. Then, in a big flood, their homes would be in danger.

Flood Prediction

Predicting floods is as important as protecting against them. We can work out when rivers are likely to overflow and when heavy rain will fall. We can tell when **storm surges** and **tsunamis** will arrive. This helps people prepare for floods and leave the area safely.

▲ A scientist checks the level of water in a river to find out how the flood water is moving.

Keeping an eye on conditions

Weather forecasts tell us how much rain to expect. This is vital for predicting floods. Rainfall is measured with a **rain gauge**. Scientists use computers to work out from the rainfall and local conditions whether a flood will happen.

Flood warnings

People are warned about likely floods on the television, radio and websites. The warnings tell people how serious the flood may be and how likely it is to happen. Warnings of flash floods are given if very heavy rain is expected.

Predicting coastal floods

Cyclones and tsunamis often cause coastal floods. Scientists work out when they will hit land, how high the storm surge will be and how much flooding it will cause. The Pacific Tsunami Warning System looks out for tsunamis. It uses **satellites** and sensors to track them. A similar system is being built for the Indian Ocean.

GLOBAL WARMING AND FLOODS

The Earth is getting hotter. This is called **global warming**. It is making the weather change and melting ice near the north and south poles. The melting ice runs into the sea and raises sea levels. Global warming also seems to cause more cyclones. Coastal floods will be more common and more serious in the future.

▲ Lines marked on buildings and bridges show how deep floods have been in the past.

TEN OF THE DEADLIEST FLOODS

When	Where	Why	Casualties
1931	China	river flood	about 3 million
1959	China	river flood	about 2 million
1970	Bangladesh	cyclone	about 500,000
1939	China	river flood	about 500,000
2004	South Asia	tsunami	283,000
1991	Bangladesh	cyclone	130,000
1815	Indonesia	tsunami	90,000
1883	Indonesia	tsunami	36,000
1963	Italy	dam overtopped	2,000
1953	Netherlands	storm surge	1,487

FURTHER INFORMATION

Books

Awesome Forces of Nature: Raging Floods by Richard and Louise Spilsbury (Heinemann, 2003)

In Time of Need: Flood by S Connolly (Franklin Watts, 2004)

Natural Disasters: Floods by Chris Oxlade (Wayland, 2007)

Our Violent Earth: Floods by Nicola Barber (Wayland, 2001)

Websites

www.bbc.co.uk/weather/features/understanding/deluges.shtml

www.environment-agency.gov.uk/subjects/flood/

geology.com/articles/tsunami-map.shtml

www.geol.ucsb.edu/faculty/sylvester/Teton%20Dam/welcome_dam.html

www.geoprojects.co.uk/Keyfile/KeyBoscastle.htm

www.pbs.org/wgbh/nova/orleans/proo-nf.html

GLOSSARY

barrage — An artificial barrier across a river that can be closed to stop a tidal surge from flowing inland.

climate change — Changes to weather patterns and temperature around the world.

cloudburst — A sudden, violent rainstorm.

cyclone — A violent tropical storm with very fast, destructive whirling winds.

delta — A fan-shaped area of land formed by sediment where a river meets the sea.

dyke — An earth bank along a river or coast designed to stop water from flooding the land.

erode — Wear away.

estuary — The final section of a large river, where fresh water from the river mixes with seawater.

evaporate — Turn from liquid to vapour.

floodplain — The area around a river that is covered with water when the river floods. It has rich soil built up from matter left behind in earlier floods.

global warming — The slow warming of the air, land and sea caused by heat trapped near the Earth by a layer of gases made when people burn fuels.

groundwater — Water that has soaked into the ground and is trapped there.

levee — An artificial embankment built alongside a river to prevent flooding of the surrounding land.

malaria — A disease carried by mosquitoes, which breed in stagnant water.

monsoon — A pattern of weather that brings a period of heavy rain.

paddy — A field for growing rice, which is kept very wet.

rain gauge — An instrument that measures the amount of rain that falls.

reservoir — A large body of water kept to provide water to towns and cities.

run-off — Water that flows over the land instead of soaking in.

satellite — A spacecraft that orbits the Earth.

saturated — Containing so much water that no more can be soaked up.

sediment — Small pieces of rock carried down a river by flowing water.

storm surge — A large wave of water that is carried inland by a violent storm.

tropical — Relating to the area of the tropics, near the equator.

tsunami — A wave caused by an earthquake, volcanic eruption or landslide.

water cycle — The path of water through various states as it falls as rain, collects in the ground or in rivers, passes through plants and animals, and evaporates from land and sea to form clouds.

water table — The top layer of groundwater.

INDEX

Page numbers in **bold** refer to illustrations.

Australia **7, 19**

Bangladesh **20**, 21, 30
Biblical flood 5

China 9, 17, 30
cloudbursts 10, 31
coastal floods 4, 12–13, 14, 15, **15**, 21, 22, 27, 29
coasts 4, 12, 13, 14, 15, **15**, 19, 21, 22, 26
cyclones 9, **9**, 12, 21, 29, 30, 31

dams 16, **16**, 17, **26**
deltas 19, 21, 31
deserts 10, **11**, 19, **19**
disease 24, 25

earthquakes 4, 14, 15, 17
erosion 6, 18, **18**, 22, 31

farming 5, 20, 21, **21**, 23, 24
flash floods 4, 10–11, **10**, **11**, 18, **18**, 19, 22, 24, 28
flood barriers 13, 26, 27, **27**
    barrages 27, 31
    dykes 13, 27, 31
    levees 26, 31
floodplains 7, **7**, 18, 19, 20, 21, 26, 27
flood prediction 28–29
flood protection 16, 26–27
floods
    Asian tsunami (2004) 15
    Bangladesh (1991) 21
    Boscastle, UK (2004) 11

China (1931) 9, 30
New Orleans, USA (2005) **5**, 13, **13**, 25
St Francis Dam, USA (1928) 17
flood warnings 28

Germany **4**, 17
global warming 16, 29, 31
groundwater 7, 31

human-made floods 16–17

India **8**, 15, **17**
Indian Ocean **9**, 15
Indonesia 14, **15**, 30
Italy **12**, 13, 30

Japan **16**, 17

landslides 14, **14**, 18

monsoons **8**, 9, 21, 31

Netherlands 13, 27, 30

plants 19, **19**, 20, 21

rain 4, 6, 8, 9, 10, 11, 18, 28
rescue 24, **24**, 25
reservoirs 17, 26, **26**, 31
river floods 4, 7, 8–9, 18, 19, 20, 21
rivers 4, **4**, 5, 6–9, **6**, **7**, 10, 11, 16, 17, 18, 19, 20, 21, 26, 27, **28**
run-off 6, 19, 31
Russia **22**

sea 4, 6, **6**, 12, 13, 21, 22, 27
sediment 19, 20, 31
South Asia 30
South-East Asia 8
Sri Lanka 15
storms 4, 9, 10, 12
storm surges 12, 13, 27, 28, 29, 30, 31
Switzerland **18**

Thailand 15
tsunamis 14–15, **14**, **15**, 19, 22, 28, 29, 30, 31
Turkey **10**

United Kingdom 11, 12, **27**
USA **5**, **11**, 13, **13**, 17, 24, 25, **25**

Vietnam **21**

water cycle 6, **6**, 31
water table 7, 31